GLOSSOLALIA

GLOSSO

POEMS BY MARITA DACHSEL

LALIA

Keymen,
keep sweet!
Marita Dachsel
Russell's opening
May 14, 2013

anvil
PRESS

Anvil Press | Canada

Library and Archives Canada Cataloguing in Publication

Dachsel, Marita
    Glossolalia / Marita Dachsel.

Poems.
ISBN: 978-1-927380-40-6

    1. Smith, Joseph, 1805-1844--Marriage--Poetry. I. Title.

    PS8557.A263G56 2012   C811'.54   C2012-905928-5

Cover design: Rayola.com
Cover image: Maggie Taylor
Interior design: Heimat House
Author photo: Nancy Lee

Represented in Canada by the Literary Press Group.

Distributed in Canada by Publishers Group Canada and in the U.S. by Small Press Distribution (SPD).

The publisher gratefully acknowledges the financial assistance of the Canada Council for the Arts, the Canada Book Fund, and the Province of British Columbia through the B.C. Arts Council and the Book Publishing Tax Credit.

Anvil Press Publishers Inc.
P.O. Box 3008, Main Post Office
Vancouver, B.C. V6B 3X5 Canada
www.anvilpress.com

Printed and bound in Canada

any real religion is a big slow poem,
while a poem is a small fast religion
— Les Murray

For Kevin

CONTENTS

Wife. Wife. Wife. Wife. Wife. Wife. Wife.
Wife. Wife. Wife. Wife. Wife. Wife. Wife.
Wife. Wife. Wife.   Wife. Wife. Wife.
Wife. Wife. Wife. Wife. Wife. Wife. Wife.
Wife. Wife. Wife. Wife. Wife. Wife. Wife.

DOCTRINE AND COVENANTS 132, 1-3

1 Verily, thus saith the Lord unto you my servant Joseph, that inasmuch as you have inquired of my hand to know and understand wherein I, the Lord, justified my servants Abraham, Isaac, and Jacob, as also Moses, David and Solomon, my servants, as touching the principle and doctrine of their having many wives and concubines—

2 Behold, and lo, I am the Lord thy God, and will answer thee as touching this matter.

3 Therefore, prepare thy heart to receive and obey the instructions which I am about to give unto you; for all those who have this law revealed unto them must obey the same.

Emma Hale Smith: One

I had no intention of marrying when I left home.
Preferring to marry him to any other man I knew, I consented.

Our thighs pressed
into each other as the wagon hiccupped
across the border.

Twice asked,
twice my father
rejected consent.
Disowned.

I regret nothing.

I am your sacrament.
Sip me.   I am your wine

*

You used to say I looked beautiful
pregnant.   It was true.
But my babies were buried
at a rate I considered labouring
squatted over a muddy hole.

Words shouldn't need context
but there is a grander world in every thing—
that watch, this broom, laundry hung to dry.

How can a lifetime fill a page?

LOUISA BEAMAN

April. A grove of elms
still, budding, poised
to hook absent clouds.
The Mississippi swells,
steeping the shores damp.
Glorious. My wedding day sparks.

At the door, my escorts hand me
a hat & cloak of my betrothed.
Now veiled as a man, a figure
safe from glimpses of the uninitiated
viewing beyond the trees.
The morning wasted with pins & curls,
my beauty crushed.

I am the sole woman
encircled by chimney-top men
who fake solemnity, shuffle giddy.
For that moment, I am a man
marrying a man, married
to a woman who is not me.

My dream—a new dress
of rustling silk
the colour of the winter sky.

Should be thankful
not to have wasted
time & money on
sewing & notions.

A sharp ember is
burned on this day—
on some occasions
a woman needs to feel
pretty to feel loved.

ELIZABETH DAVIS GOLDSMITH BRACKENBURY DURFEE

Blackmail is an ugly word.
I don't like it
& it wasn't really blackmail.
No, I'd say it was more
an expression of knowledge,
of consequences.
The bigger picture.

We had an agreement:
I wouldn't tell his wife
as long as he made me his,
and I helped recruit. No,
wait, that's too strong.
Persuade? Yes. Persuade
some of the younger girls.

Don't look at me that way.
I am proud of what I did,
a woman of my age, my status.
Anyone would have done the same.
Foolish not to.

FANNY ALGER

Emma's fired up.

Keeps complaining about how I miss the corners sweeping,
don't move stuff dusting.

I try. I do. It's just so hard,
so hard to do anything feeling this way.
Lunch always rises up, lodged at the top of my throat.
I want to puke every breath of the day.
Or sleep.
But a hired girl can't sleep the day away.

I hate it when she's mad at me.
I love her. I do. I love her.

But Joseph's the one whispering his in the middle of the night.
Sneaks in like a cat, hopping on my bed
all hands & breath & mewing release.

I'd much rather be in her arms.
Not in that way of course, but you know. Like a daughter.

I wish I hadn't agreed to be his wife, 16 was too young.
It's been a whole year now.

God, just the thought of eggs makes me want to hurl.

Reckon the living of it was merely the living of it.
Nothing spectacular.

Well, bless your heart.
Of course.
The husbands.
No one is interested my childhood.
Attention is always shined on the men.

                              Fine. Allow me:
Wm Morgan: 27 yrs my sr,
            Fathered my children.
            Enjoyed a dram or 2.
(ignore the propaganda, he was not an alcoholic)
            Died an anti-Mason martyr.

Yes, a martyr.

Geo. Harris: 21 yrs my sr
            Charismatic. Convert.
            Masonic & Mormon leader.
            Ended in divorce.
            He died a yr later.

Jos. Smith: 4 yrs my jr
            Vivacious. Magnetic.
            Had a living wife.
            I had a living husband.
            Died a Mormon martyr.

Yes, another martyr. But you were already aware of that.
(Men & their divisions. Always eager for a reason to fight.)

It was simple: love & marriage. No.
What a word. Why should I be sad?
I have known devotion. Deeply.
That's why I had to leave Nauvoo.

Here I am, in Tennessee
of all places, now a Sister of Charity.
The war is killing the souls of our country
& someone has to nurse them back to health.

PATTY BARTLETT SESSIONS

I

I was 17, newly married
when I first put a woman to bed,
her new babe in arms.

Awaiting death, I've tallied,
attended 3977 births. Midwife,
my eminent title.

Pride is a sin,
but I think I will be forgiven
for the surge I feel
when I consider my record.

II

47 did not feel old,
but looked ancient to him.
A month after my daughter,
me. Sexless, righteous.
Virtuous. Finished.

III

I became a Mother in Israel,
coaxing young women
into the new covenant.

We were Sarah & Hagar. Rachel & Leah.

But I was wrong about polygamy.

Lust, envy & wrath are sins,
& I know I will never be forgiven
for being the zealous handmaiden
to this difficult life.

IV

I have lost four children. Heartache
is my chronic companion,
chafing the every day.

But my dear husband David
took a second wife
& I will tell you
what the others won't admit:

There is no other earthly pain,
constant, raw & rending,
like sharing your man
with a younger wife.

V

I am a practical woman:
I can heal with herbs & my hands,
I brew my own beer, sew, knit,
& speak in tongues.

After birth, I would show
the mother the slick placenta,
raised up, a stretched orb.
An offering.

It carries the tree of life.
Rough, ropey. Red,
the colour of strawberry jam
boiling low on the stove.

VI

Being the first hand
to touch a life
is a powerful thing.

I have wondered
what imprint
I have left

& what has been
left on me.

Ruth Daggett Vose Sayers

I believed it was his fever talking, hot & delusional,
but even after it broke & he was back to day-to-day living,
he'd return to those words that pocked:

                                        I feel sorry for you.

He said that my Edward was a fine man, but not a Saint
& I would be nobody's queen
in the next life. He said I was too good to be alone.
I could join him in the celestial kingdom.

Edward was baffled by all this. He often was when it came to the Church.

We agreed that it was kind of Joseph to think of me, include me in his plans
& that maybe he just wanted to thank us for keeping him
safe & hidden from the mobs
& for nursing him back. Really, it was the least he could do.

But Edward said he could not follow how a woman with two husbands
would be more Christly than with just one.
He said that I was a fine woman, the best
& that he'd consent if I promised to stay with him and pray for his soul.

He said he never understood the ways of God.
I told him, neither did I.

OLIVE GREY FROST

How to get rid of bed bugs:

1. Put a drop of mercury in a tumbler.
2. Add the white of two eggs.
3. Mix together.
4. Apply to bed with a feather.

Look at this. Bites
up & down my body.
Didn't know what they were
until one of the Sisters pulled me aside.
Wish the others had the sense
to tell me at the beginning. Sure,
there was plenty to remember,
but something practical
would have been much appreciated.

Nauvoo

The land jutted out,
like an obstinate chin.
It was a sponge soaking
in the woeful Mississippi.

Ague plagued
every Spring. Chills
and fevers lingered,
stained for life.

The land, the mosquitoes,
transformed by the hand of man,
the will of God. Once a soggy hell,
soon rivalled Chicago in size.

DOCTRINE AND COVENANTS 132, 19-21

19 And again, verily I say unto you, if a man marry a wife by my word, which is my law, and by the new and everlasting covenant, and it is sealed unto them by the Holy Spirit of a promise, by him who is anointed, unto whom I have appointed this power and the keys of this priesthood; and it shall be said unto them—Ye shall come forth in the first resurrection; and if it be after the first resurrection, in the next resurrection; and shall inherit thrones, kingdoms, principalities, and powers, dominions, all heights and depths— then shall it be written in the Lamb's Book of Life, that he shall commit no murder whereby to shed innocent blood, and if ye abide in my covenant, and commit no murder whereby to shed innocent blood, it shall be done unto them in all things whatsoever my servant hath put upon them, in time, and through all eternity; and shall be of full force when they are out of the world; and they shall pass by the angels, and the gods, which are set there, to their exaltation and glory in all things, as hath been sealed upon their heads, which glory shall be a fullness and a continuation of the seeds forever and ever.

20 Then shall they be gods, because they have no end; therefore shall they be from everlasting to everlasting, because they continue; then shall they be above all, because all things are subject unto them. Then shall they be gods, because they have all power, and the angels are subject to them.

21 Verily, verily I say unto you, except ye abide my law ye cannot attain to this glory.

Hannah Ells

My life:

I live a boring life in a boring house
with my boring boring. I am a boring
seamstress and boring boring boring.
Boring am a boring of the Boring Boring.
I am boring because of boring boring
that boring boring boring figure.
I boring boring it.

My after-life:

Promises to be extraordinary.

DELCENA DIADAMIA JOHNSON SHERMAN

His floods. His tornadoes.
Plagues. Drought.

Over nothing.
It's never personal.

A cracked bowl. Torn pants.
Dropped food. Smeared shit.

Five crisp crescents
on a chubby thigh;

a taut hairbrush;
a smothering embrace;

a clumsy constellation
from rough diaper pins.

A mother has only
so much patience,

so much time
to clean & care,

for goodly work.
God knows.

I forgive
His outbursts

of destruction
& damage.

I understand
prayers ignored

cried out
in a cold night

needing to suckle,
desperate in faith.

Presendia Lathrop Huntington Buell

My ululations have scraped across this country,
my voice, like fingers grieved to the bone,
leaving grooves thick enough for wagon wheels.

I would follow any man who promised our reunions,
who gave me no blame, who understood completely
when I sensed them

                        as shadows between the trees
                        glints in the rushing brook
                        antelope racing our wagon.

My back turned, I am a lunatic.
Stories of mine retold—the angels pacing,
my own children visiting—easy in lightness.

I repeat their names aloud: Silas. Thomas.
                        Chauncy. Adaline. John.
                        Presendia Celestia.

If I don't continue to mother them,
give their names breath,
no one ever will.

Silas, Thomas, Chauncy, Adaline, John, Presendia Celestia,
Silas, Thomas, Chauncy, Adaline, John, Presendia Celestia,
SilasThomasChauncyAdalineJohnPresendiaCelestia

My three other children have grown & left.
I still speak to my six, keep them close.
But they, too, have tired of me, give me no signs.

My heart is rutted like the prairie after frost.
I'd like to trace my finger along its deep scars, discover
where the furrows meet. Certain it won't be as simple as death.

FANNY YOUNG CARR MURRAY

ha ha ha ha
ha ha ha ha
ha ha ha ha
ha ha ha ha

I've read more than both those boys twinned
& their talk of necessity and exaltation
is as charming as puppies
chewing on Sunday shoes.

Now, don't talk to me; when I get into the celestial kingdom,
if I ever get there,
I shall request the privilege of being a ministering angel;
that is the labour I wish to perform.

They called me foolish,
said that I know not of what I speak.
Condescending & earnest,
a prophet's proposal lobbed to me.

Listen:
    I don't want
        any companion
            in that world.

My brother pleaded
like he was a child again.
When I conceded, their tails
would have wagged if they had them.

That moment, over tea and cookies, I was married
not for love or eternal companionship,
but because I needed to return to my beloved silence
& the dog-eared novel I had waiting beside my bed.

EMMA HALE SMITH: TWO

I believe he was everything he professed to be.

I believe I believed. Joseph,
you were everything, everything
I believed. I profess.
You believed everything.
You professed everything.
I believed you
until I couldn't.

I confess.

I lose you.
I lose you my life over.
I lost you.

*

How old am I now?
Can you tell by my voice? My hands?
The way I sigh?

A person does not lose faith—
it is not a hairpin or a tooth.
Faith evolves, salvaged.
A grove becomes a house.
A fire becomes ashes.

What will be my last thought?
My last words? Will I call to you?

ZINA DIANTHA HUNTINGTON JACOBS

his skin metallic
seeps of beer

never a binger
but a steady consumer

my saltlick areolas
his cow tongue

I sleep with strangers
four Egyptians

mummies: a patriarch
& his wives

stashed beneath
the belly of my bed

repulsion swelled
to salty gratitude

monotony spliced
eyes sealed

take me
take me back

to righteous times
most beloved

ignore hardship
cradle the unspoken

anytime is better
than the present

MARY ELIZABETH ROLLINS LIGHTNER

Joseph said I was his before I was born,
that all the Devils in hell
should never steal me from him,
& I was created for Joseph
before the foundation of Earth was laid.

Joseph said an angel came to him
three times between '34 & '42
& he was to obey
that principle or the angel
would destroy him.

Joseph said he had the oath of God upon it & God cannot lie.

Joseph said I shall have a witness, to pray
earnestly for the angel said unto him I should have a witness,
that the angel appeared & was well pleased
& I should have a witness.

Joseph said did I implore, 'Father, help me?'
& if I had, my mouth would have been opened
for verily this was an angel of the living God,
with more knowledge, intelligence & light
than ever dared to be revealed.

Joseph said I covered my face
& the angel was insulted,
but if I am faithful I shall see far greater.

Joseph said Emma thought the world of me.

Joseph said to stay with my husband Adam Lightner.

Joseph said if we attempted to leave the Church
we would endure plenty of Sorrow.
Property made on the right hand, lost on the left.
There would be sickness on sickness
& our children would be lost.

Joseph said I would have to work
harder than I had ever dreamed
& at last when I was worn out & ready to die,
I would return to the Church.

Joseph said all this to me & everything happened just as Joseph said.

SYLVIA PORTER SESSIONS LYON

Men must retire to the woods
to receive visions of God. Women
give birth & see His face,
feel Him push through.

The details of all nine births live in me,
cross-stitched to my lungs
& I can recall each one
as if they had happened this dawn.

But my dear Josephine, my fourth birth,
hers stands out amongst them all.
I knew she would be my first to live
to adulthood even before she was born.

Poor Windsor thought she was his,
but the speed & intensity of her birth confirmed
what I had surmised: she was the Prophet's
just as much as she was mine.

I wanted to ask Emma if she, too,
had felt transformed by the tearing,
exorcised & cleansed by the pain,
if euphoria brought her closer

to God, to her husband as it had me.
But there are some conversations,
even amongst mothers,
best kept in the heart.

AGNES MOULTON COOLBRITH SMITH

A knitting needle pierces the prairie night.
I swaddle myself in my marriage
quilt & lumber outside
to a crowd of smug stars.

My belly, again, too heavy.
Oh to be lithe,
fierce in movement, darning
the grasses to the edge.

I search for my husband
in the pinpricked sky. Can you see
me, Don Carlos? I miss your letters
your poetry, your gentle presence.

You knew family was not easy
& sometimes neither was faith.
You must know I am to marry Joseph.
Your words no lullaby, a nightly refrain:

Any man who will teach & practice
the doctrine of spiritual wifery
will go to hell; I don't care
if it is my brother Joseph.

Once he is gone, yet another of your clan
will take his place beside this levirate wife.
Choice is an Autumn leaf. I am limp
with questions, no place in this world.

Do you know the difference
between faith & hope?
Do you know how to live
with one, but not the other?

I do. I do.

sweep wipe spin weave plant cook sick well
garden tend harvest prepare turn preserve
render produce tallow lard candles soap
carry water carry water carry water three
meals dishes laundry mend sew body soul
one cast iron stove pious pure domestic
submissive pious pure domestic

51 Verily, I say unto you: A commandment I give unto mine handmaiden, Emma Smith, your wife, who I have given unto you, that she stays herself and partake not of that which I commanded you to offer unto her; for I did it, saith the Lord, to prove you all, as I did Abraham, and that I might require an offering at your hand, be covenant and sacrifice.

52 And let mine handmaiden, Emma Smith, receive all those that have been given unto my servant Joseph, and who are virtuous and pure before me; and those who are not pure, and have said they were pure, shall be destroyed, saith the Lord God.

53 For I am the Lord thy God, and ye shall obey my voice; and I give unto my servant Joseph that he shall be made ruler over many things; for he hath been faithful over a few things, and from henceforth I will strengthen him.

54 And I command mine handmaiden, Emma Smith, to abide and cleave unto my servant Joseph, and to none else. But if she will not abide this commandment she shall be destroyed, saith the Lord; for I am the Lord thy God, and I will destroy her if she abide not in my law.

55 But if she will not abide this commandment, then shall my servant Joseph do all things for her, even as he hath said; and I will bless him and multiply him and give him an hundredfold in this world, of fathers and mothers, brothers and sisters, houses and lands, wives and children, and crowns of eternal lives in the eternal worlds.

56 And again, verily I say, let mine handmaiden forgive my servant Joseph his trespasses; and then shall she be forgiven her trespasses, wherein she has trespassed against me; and I, the Lord thy God, will bless her, and multiply her, and make her heart to rejoice.

ALMERA WOODWARD JOHNSON

He creeps in

He creeps in   I pretend to sleep

I pretend to sleep   shift night shift

I pretend to sleep   shift night shift   wiggle against his lap

shift night shift   wiggle against his lap   hand

shift wiggle lap   hand on hip

on hip   hip to belly

hand on hip to belly to breast

to breast   heavy in his palm

breast heavy in his palm   fingers

palm breast   fingers vice

fingers vice   vice from breast

breast to ribs   breast to ribs to hip

breast to ribs to hip to thigh

hip to thigh   hip to thigh

fingers hip to thigh to quim   to quim   fingers to quim

quim to fingers   roll over   roll

over quim to fingers to mouth to lips to   over mouth

over mouth to fingers to lips to tongue   over tongue quim over

fingers lips tongue over lips tongue quim tongue fingers mouth lips

over to   over to   over

EMILY DOW PARTRIDGE

Keep walking. Keep walking, don't think about it. Don't think

about this morning, being deep in the washing when Mrs. Durfee stopped by,
telling me to meet him tonight at the Kimballs'. Couldn't change
my dress, people would wonder, so here I am stinking of sweat and lye
walking as fast as I can, walking away from them.

Walk faster, faster, past the grocer's, round the corner, out of view. Stop thinking

of how I go to the Kimballs' as instructed. Only Helen & her older brother William
are there, looking at me like I'm part loon showing up after dark,
then their father, Brother Heber, arrives with Joseph, both dithering.
Kids weren't supposed to be there, awake, no one but the two men & me.
Everyone's confused,

but me. Don't look back.

Heber says it's late & his wife's not at home, so come visit another time.
Like it's an ordinary visit, like I'm the one in the wrong.
Sends the children to a neighbour & me back home.

Faster. He's calling me back. Pretend I don't hear.

I'm still walking, walking as fast as I can.
This is my chance. I'm being saved from the madness.
Got to getaway, getaway. Six blocks and I'm saved.

ELIZA MARIA PARTRIDGE

Emma places my hand in his. Her hand is cold pastry.
Barely a touch, her gesture a whisper. Looks like she's going to faint.
No clue that we've been married already for two months.
Ninny chose Emily & me because she thinks we're safe.
The moment it is over, she runs out of the room to throw up or cry.

*

Hours after the ceremony, she demands our divorce & every day after that.
Whoa, lady.
We were part of a sacred covenant—you can't just snap your fingers
& have that be gone. See you in eternity, Sister.

Hang on, as matter of fact—snap, snap—Emma can.

*

Months later in Emma's room, Joseph stands hang-dogged, martyr-like.
She says blood will flow.
Eyes roll,
we hear this almost every day for months. She tells us to marry someone else.
Not interested, thank you very much.

But it is over. Joseph offers his warm mitt, heavy & firm like a large peach.
Our divorce, a handshake.

*

Town's all atwitter over Joseph running for President, as if he stands a chance. Haven't spoken to him since we were flicked out of his house after Emma threatened divorce. Theirs is a love I'll never understand.

Nor this political campaign.

How can a man control a country if he can't control his wife?

If any Smith could run this country, I'd put my money on Emma, hands down.

Anonymous

[she is still
head turned
face mirrored
in the window

powdery pale
a pink flash
erupts
from collar
to temples

dry lips
thin
anchored

lifts teacup
sees it empty
returns to saucer
contemplates
tea leaves

& speaks:]

        I have nothing
        to say to you.

EMMA HALE SMITH: THREE

I did not ask for this life but accept it as my calling.

I have watched you dance, ignored
how close your lips—
how firm your palms—
where your fingers—
ignored them all.

Salacious whispers carry far:
How can one woman create such change?
How can one man?

*

You stalked home,
witching hour, stinking.
Their perfumed sex
soiling our bed.

Melancholy marrow.
Too much silence.
My heart is as ripe as yours.

What I know: not all eggshells are fragile.
Not all twigs snap.

I wanted
what they
had: him.   His love.
                 His love.
                 His love.   & oh,
                                         those
                                       hands.

Helped to
the help,
him to them.   I had what,
                 was what,
                 he wanted.   Youth.
                                       In his home.
                                       Willing. Easy.

& so
I sang,   transformed
                 to a songbird,   (lilting, territorial,
                                       with intent)

at every
opportunity—   parties,
                 performances   political
                                       platforms.

His ear.
                 His eye.

                                       Him.

Desdemona Caitlin Wadsworth Fullmer

Hands ruined bleaching cloth so white even angels would avert their eyes.

Emma despised the suit and me for making it—
the acquisition of exact measurements take time and precision.

She refused to entertain the sacrifice of my hard work.

I exiled myself from their domicile,
abandoned the rich food, crisp linens & beloved friends
because I give credence to premonitions

& our husband confirmed the verity of mine.
Emma could be the death of me:

sipping tea & poisoned unsuspectingly as I darned her stockings
& she hummed at the pages of her book.

MARINDA NANCY JOHNSON HYDE

& these are my tomatoes
planted 24 varieties this year
been collecting seeds, trading
for almost a decade

here I feel
            like a patriarch
fingers splayed, laying hands
blessing the rows

like a wife, these plants respond
well to attention, a gentle sweep
of the leaves, tickle of the flower
& they won't stop giving

now,
            bring your palms to your face,
inhale
            oh, that smell

can you imagine?
after all these years
I still can't find the right words
to describe their scent

FLORA ANN WOODWORTH

I

Orange Wight
came courting

gawky & awkward
18 & with prospects

& when I walked with him
I could see myself

a wife proper
a mother & a good life

II

O at first
it was fun

until Emma showed up
hysterical & desperate

scratched at my skin
to remove the watch

a gift from my
husband & hers

III

O was it fun
even at first

Orange Wight shamed me
for leading him on

& when my husband died
I was left with

nothing
not even secrets

THE TEMPLE

Exquisite day. Breathe it in:
chest hurts, nostrils freeze.
The world white & simple,
no line between ground & sky.

On the hill, stone rises.
The men fortify, air
cluttered with their busyness.
Every hour the Temple emerges.

Joseph runs for President.
Spring will return early this year,
a fervent green. Another
spongy season ripe for ague.

61 And again, as pertaining to the law of the priesthood—if any man espouse a virgin, and desire to espouse another, and the first give her consent, and if he espouse the second, and they are virgins, and have vowed to no other man, then is he justified; he cannot commit adultery for they are given unto him; for he cannot commit adultery with that that belongeth unto him and to no one else.

62 And if he have ten virgins given unto him by this law, he cannot commit adultery, for they belong to him, and they are given unto him; therefore he is justified.

63 But if one or either of the ten virgins, after she is espoused, shall be with another man, she has committed adultery, and shall be destroyed; for they are given unto him to multiply and replenish the earth, according to my commandment, and to fulfil the promise which was given by my Father before the foundation of the world, and for their exaltation in the eternal worlds, that they may bear the souls of men; for herein is the work of my father continued, that he may be glorified.

64 And again, verily, verily, I say unto you, if any man have a wife, who holds the keys of this power, and he teaches unto her the law of my priesthood as pertaining to these things, then shall she believe and administer unto him, or she shall be destroyed, saith the Lord your God; for I will destroy her; for I will magnify my name upon all those who receive and abide in my laws.

HELEN MAR KIMBALL

Instructed to create a dynasty,
for eternity only.
(Only! If only, only.)
Nope. For time, too.

This time.
Now time.
Time with his hands,
time against his oily skin,
time wetted by his tuba mouth,
time cooped under his barrelled body,
time scratching against his encroaching hair.

*

I am sick of God
& his trials & tests.
I am sick of Joseph
playing the same games.

Faith has worn me out.

*

My mother suffered.
A church widow,
a wife sacrificing
for the greater good.

*

My father traded me
for a promise
of eternal salvation.

I was second prize.

Joseph almost had my mother,
chattelled for the offering.
But she was not a trinket
to be palmed
from one clammy hand
to another.

Behold! He claimed his demand was a test.
Ye olde Abraham & Sarah & the Pharaoh trick.
Glad handing, back slapping, I love you manning.

I'm still surprised she didn't kill them both then & there.

*

On good days,
days of big faith & calm heartedness,

I convince
myself my father
was Abraham
& I am Isaac.

*

Hear this:
Abraham was a coward.
Sarah was a bitch.

My daily gratitude:
Lot & his appalling family
were never an interest.

*

Yea, I rejoice
at the news
of his death.

There is a boy I love
who loves me.
We will marry.
This time, for time,
I will know joy.

ELVIRA ANNIE COWLES HOLMES

Who?
Oh. No.

Well, no.

We—

Well. Well, we. We—

Own? No.
Woe? No.
Owe? No.
No. No. No.

Loon? Eel?
Hen, ewe?
Ew, no.

No.

One: lone, hollow, wee, woollen.

Ween we: we wheel, we howl,
new, whole. We woo,

hone, hewn.

One. We wow.
We won.

SARAH ANN WHITNEY

Here's one: what does a bride wear at her pretend marriage to her uncle?
I know, a classic question, right? One for the ages.

I blame my mother.

She's been way too involved from day one. Even before day one, arranging
with glee my marriage to Joe, standing proud on our wedding day, like some
over-zealous stage-mother. I'm the first to have her mother at the
so-called secret ceremony. How embarrassing.

He's had a pretty busy time these last few months, hiding everywhere from
Montrose to Warsaw. The mobs really have it in for him. But my mother,
oh she won't let the mobs "stand in the way of her daughter." No way.
Escorted me all over Illinois so I could "comfort" him.

Then she started with the math. Tallies and graphs and charts. Figures I
should be with child by now. With child? I'm still in school, for crying out
loud.

But she doesn't want to be a grandmother. Not really. Not yet. She's miffed
that I don't have the status she thinks I, but really she, deserves. Thinks if
I'm the first of the wives to have his spawn, I'll suddenly have rank. She
knows Miss Snow and the Partridge girls are married & in his house.
Wants me to have the same.

No thanks.

It's not working out for her at all. Last time we saw him she ever so slightly implied that maybe, perhaps, I might be in a delicate way. Unbelievable. I denied it, of course. Who lies to a prophet? My mother, that's who.

Joseph's unnerved & made some arrangements. So now I'm about to be married off to my Uncle Joseph. Yeah, another Joseph. How many Josephs can one girl handle? My dad's sister passed away six months ago, and now I'm taking her place. Gag. He's already promised all this is fake, that there won't be any "comforting" going on. I don't care. It's all so gross. But at least I'll be out of my mother's house. Now that's a silver lining.

Lucy Walker

I

~~When at length we were forced to believe she would not speak to us~~
~~again we were in the depths of despair. Ten motherless children! &~~
~~such a young mother! The youngest not yet two years old. The~~
~~Prophet came to the rescue. He said, if you~~ **remain** ~~here Brother~~
~~Walker, you will soon~~ **follow** ~~your wife. You must have a~~ **change** ~~of~~
~~scene, a~~ **change** ~~of climate. You have just such a family as I could~~
~~love. My house shall be their home. For the present, I would advise~~
~~you to sell your effects, place the little ones with kind friends, & the~~
~~four eldest shall come to my house & be~~ **received** ~~& treated as my~~
~~own children, & if I find the little ones are not content, or not treat-~~
~~ed right, I will bring them home & keep them   thought   of~~
~~being broken up as a family, & being separated from the little ones.~~
~~However my father sought to~~ **comfort** ~~us by saying two years~~
~~would soon pass by when with renewed health he hoped to~~ **return**
~~& make us a home where we might be together again. The tears~~
~~rained down our faces all the while we were with them — the peo-~~
~~ple often said they wished we would~~ **calm** ~~ourselves in their pres-~~
~~ence or not come to see them as it made them discontented~~.

'I have a message for you, I have been commanded of God to take another wife, & you are the woman.' My astonishment knew no bounds. This announcement was indeed a thunderbolt to me. He asked me if I believed him to be a Prophet of God. 'Most assuredly I do,' I replied. He fully explained to me the principle of plural or celestial marriage. Said this principle was again to be restored for the benefit of the human family. That it would prove an everlasting blessing to my father's house. & form a chain that could never be broken, worlds without end. Oh that the grave would kindly receive me that I might find rest on the bosom of my dear mother. Why - Why should I be chosen from among thy daughters, Father, I am only a child in years and experience. Not mother to council; no father near to tell me what to do, in this trying hour. Oh let this bitter cup pass. & this I prayed in the agony of my soul. "It is a command of God to you. I will give you until tomorrow to decide this matter. If you reject this message the gate will be closed forever against you." This aroused every drop of Scotch in my veins. I felt at this moment that I was called to place myself upon the altar of a living sacrifice, perhaps to brook the world in disgrace and incur the displeasure & contempt of my youthful companions; all my dreams of happiness blow to the four winds, this was too much, the thought was unbearable. I emphatically forbid him speaking again to me on this Subject. With the most beautiful expression of countenance, & said, 'God almighty bless you, you shall have a manifestation of the will of God concerning you; a testimony that you can never deny. I will tell you what it shall be. It shall be that peace & joy that you never knew.

III

~~My room became~~ filled ~~with~~ a ~~heavenly influence. To me it was in comparison like the brilliant sun~~ bursting ~~though the darkest~~ cloud ~~...My soul was filled with calm, sweet peace that I never knew. Supreme happiness took possession of my whole being. & I received a powerful & irrastible testimony of the truth of the marriage covenant called 'celestial or plural marriage.' Which has been like an~~ anchor ~~to the soul through all the trials of life. I felt that I must go out into~~ the morning air ~~& give~~ vent ~~to the joy & gratitude that filled my soul. As I descended the stairs, President Smith opened the door below; took me by the hand & said: 'Thank God, you have the testimony. I too, have prayed.' He led me to a chair, placed his hands upon my head, & blessed me with every blessing my heart could possibly desire. It was not a love matter, so to~~ speak~~, in our affairs—at least on my part it was not, but simply the giving~~ of ~~myself as a~~ sacrifice ~~to establish that~~ grand & glorious ~~principle that God had revealed to the world.~~

                 I am a woman. My sister

is just a kid.   thinks I'm just a kid.

                 She won't let me

                 have my own life.

                 We share everything.

                 First as children:

dresses, shoes, bonnets, books, a dollhouse, rocking horse, rolling hoop,

Papa's affection,   Mama's attention.

                 then Papa's inheritance.

                 Even Emma

can't tell us apart   keeps us together

                 allowing Joseph

                 to marry us both.

She's not stupid.   She's so stupid.

                 Thanks to that lusty sum

                 first we're adopted

                 & then betrothed.

                 Now we share:

his fears of death,   his freshly shaved

neck,

his childhood memories,   his peachy lobe,

his uncomfortable dreams.   his muscled thigh.

                 My sister is jealous of me.

I'm the one named   She's the one named

                 in his arrest warrant.

                 I'm the one

who will   who won't

                 be remembered.

Rhoda Richards

My heart lives in this box.
Open it.

A sturdy straw nest with woven layers of grass & hair. Such fine
craftsmanship. Can a person say that about a bird? Is it craft or
instinct? As a child I made straw bonnets. They were once very
fashionable, but no longer. Like most things it seems, fashions
come and go. I haven't tried for years, I'm sure I've now forgotten,
another loss.

Four eggs. I still don't know what colour they are. River-ice blue?
With brown freckles. I saw a rock once, turquoise I believe, its
colour was close to these eggs, but far more vibrant. I don't think
I've ever seen a shade this colour. Maybe it's the colour of heaven?
It's the colour of these eggs, but the name Chipping Sparrow Blue
won't be catching on I'm sure.

I am ninety-four, much too old to still be shuffling on this earth.
The nest is seventy. Why isn't it dust?

Every New Year's Eve, the anniversary of Ebenezer's death, I take
it out and cradle it. We were to be married, this was his gift to
me, a promise of what we were to have. I don't grieve either of
my husbands, Joseph or Brigham, but the one who should have
been, whose hands retrieved this perfect symbol, whose mouth
carefully emptied the shells of life. In my mind's eye I can see
him climbing the white pine, already too old for such antics.

71

I was fifty-eight when I married Joseph. He was busy collecting pretty young wives, only married me for my brother Willard. Willard wanted to start collecting spiritual wives, too. I was an offering, a way of connecting the families. I don't know why the men didn't just marry each other. Seems like that's what they really wanted, to be tied together for eternity. But I suppose that's considered a sin.

Then Brigham married me, something about strengthening the family bonds, reckoned I needed someone to care for me, but he's my first cousin so I was family anyway and family is supposed to take care of each other. In heaven, there's so much crisscrossing of family lines, bound to be a big old messy knot, a rat's nest they call it. I don't know, I've never seen a rat's nest. Either way, it'll be untidy. I've never been untidy, mother made sure we knew how to keep house at a very young age. I still sweep twice a day. Keeps a woman honest.

Ebenezer is in Heaven. Took care of that. Had a nephew do a Baptism of the Dead way back in the Nauvoo days in the Mississippi. Poor fellow got ague. Didn't die thankfully. I've been thinking that maybe in Heaven Joseph will let me be with Ebenezer. Joe's got plenty of wives and I won't be bringing any children to add to his kingdom. He won't miss me. I'm one small straw in his sprawling nest.

I love this nest more than anything else. It is a miracle it's still intact. But I must admit when I look at it, those four emptied eggs, I wonder how many generations vanished with his promise. One future traded for another.

MARTHA McBRIDE KNIGHT

The air smelled like honey,
the day warm & heavy.

I was bread rising
for thick hands to shape.

*

Bed stripped, sheets rolled
around my fists.

My whitest linens,
my finest embroidery

witness to two marriages
consummated, two men loved.

Anguish, steam
scalding my throat,

I wanted the best
of me to cover him,

cloak his death.
Be the last to lie with him.

*

I am not used to this,
how the land goes on forever,

chokes me with space,
its immensity.

I will never see New England again,
its ragged, stony hem,

the burning lace
of autumn.

I am now corseted in a life of exile.
Unleaven, caught.

AFTER THE MARTYRDOM

The men, they surged
from their homes,
from their women,
a confluence
in search of
their Galilee.

They shuffled, scuffed
dirt across the land,
a hand of a crone.

The men, they fished.
Eyes skimmed the shore
for a stranger they would know.
Hope bobbed in their throats.
Loss, a lure, caught
shredding what they once knew true.

The women, they were left
with the children,
the dead.
The scriptures gave no guide
for wives at a time like this.

I didn't know how to mourn, how to be
a widow at fifteen. Don't be confused
by my tears, my face pale & quivering
as a swallow's breast.

Blood. My first period. I didn't know
& thought sex equalled pregnancy.
All my fluttering & chirping not for the sight
of my shrouded husband but for what I'd hoped

would be a daughter with thick chocolate curls.
I wanted to build a nest, play house,
get to know the man I married, the woman
I hoped to become.

EMMA HALE SMITH: FOUR

My husband was my crown.

I mother four boys. I soothe
scrapes, calm tempers, embrace
& love & love
& love & love.

As men, one will revere life,
one will die too young, one will lead
the church, one will go mad.

Each one,
exactly like his father.

*

Simply,
I like cured ham, raspberry jam
& enjoy a strong brewed tea.

I am a new country, unfurled.
I will slay the lion. I will be the oak.
I own hope. I choose faith.

I am at home
in the spray & swell
of furious weather.

Skin split from chapping
seeks no salve.

SARAH MARYETTA KINGSLEY HOWE CLEVELAND

Not going West.
Sisters worried.
They've no reason.

I worry for them.
It's different now
since Brigham leads.

Don't trust him.
He tries to take
our power away.

Won't let us meet.
It won't work.
We've gone underground.

A woman is more
than a housekeeper,
a seamstress, a cook.

God works
through us.
to create life.

We lay our hands.
Speak in tongues.
Prophesize.

We wash & bless the sick.
Baptize the dead.
We hold the priesthood keys.

My favourite sacrament:
anointing women
heavy with child

with blessings of safety,
strength, health,
life & spirit.

He tries to stop us,
knows we're powerful.
Fool is rightly afraid.

ELIZA ROXCY SNOW

I will never feel the ache
of filling breasts
heavy for release
or the need to hide my blouse
blooming with stain,

but do not be mistaken.

I know the urgent suckle
of a needy mouth.

*

My legacy, virile:
poetess
prophetess
presidentess
priestess

A mouthful?
                    Absolutely,
Unequivocally deserved.

He & I were each other's match.
Perfectly twinned,

                        entwined.

            A circle
so ravenous for itself

                   a helix
winding to heaven.

Only Emma had found him first.

*

You might believe I care only about my legacy.
This is a rumour, a falsity,

                       but let me tell you this:
If I had to be everything to my husband,
or any person—man or child—
I would have nothing left.

Imagine me that ordinary.

Emma was a friend.
Emma was a fool.
Emma was short-sighted.
Emma could be cruel.

*

As women, we lost our chance.

Over years of washing & sun-drying
worn bare until salvaged,
ripped up for rags.

(What a waste.)

I told him
a father in heaven is a fine idea,
but don't we need a mother, too?
Every man deserves
at least one wife,
even God.

With his hand
on my thigh,
he agreed.

*

I knew she would see,
could hear the brush of her hem
along the floor
stalking her door.

I should have been afraid.

Instead, I allowed myself to be
pressed like a scented handkerchief,
his mouth less urgent
than it should have been.

I translated the voices of angels.

I have learned that the spirit
is only as powerful
as the person who holds it.

*

Fourteen steps
is a flight
of stairs.

Fourteen steps
was a flight
of life.

*

I was never destined
to be a mother

but oh how I wanted that life
which flickered in me.

My love came to me
after his death,

        when I believed
I was very near my own.

He told me to not give up,
        to not let go.

I had work to do.
Still so much to accomplish
for myself, for him.

& so I did.
& so I will
be remembered.

(Did he visit her?
        Unlikely.)

Rending. Split skin. Tears.
A flight of stairs.
A broom handle.
The door. Darkness.
Wails. Blood.
An imperceptible death.
The neighbours watching.
Unaverted.

*

There are many versions of the story,
& you should be wise enough to know
that truth is filtered through tongues.

Appendix

DATES, MARITAL STATUS, AND AGE AT MARRIAGE TO SMITH

NAME AT TIME OF MARRIAGE	MARRIAGE DATE	MARITAL STATUS	AGE
Emma Hale	January 1827	single	22
Fanny Alger	1833*	single	16
Lucinda Pendleton Morgan Harris	1838*	married	37
Louisa Beaman	April 1841	single	26
Zina Diantha Huntington Jacobs	October 1841	married	20
Presendia Lathrop Huntington Buell	December 1841	married	31
Agnes Moulton Coolbrith Smith	January 1842	widowed	33
Sylvia Porter Sessions Lyon	February 1842	married	23
Mary Elizabeth Rollins Lightner	February, 1842	married	23
Patty Bartlett Sessions	March 1842	married	47
Marinda Nancy Johnson Hyde	April 1842	married	27
Elizabeth Davis			
Goldsmith Brackenbury Durfee	June 1842*	married	50
Sarah Maryetta Kingsley Howe Cleveland	June 1842*	married	53
Delcena Diadamia Johnson Sherman	June 1842	widowed	35
Eliza Roxcy Snow	June 1842	single	38
Sarah Ann Whitney	July 1842	single	17
Martha McBride Knight	August 1842	widowed	37
Ruth Daggett Vose Sayers	February 1843	married	33
Flora Ann Woodworth	March 1843	single	16
Emily Dow Partridge	March 1843	single	19
Eliza Maria Partridge	March 1843	single	22
Almera Woodward Johnson	April 1843	single	30
Lucy Walker	May 1843	single	17
Sarah Lawrence	May 1843	single	17
Maria Lawrence	May 1843	single	19
Helen Mar Kimball	May 1843	single	14
Hannah Ells	June 1843	single	29
Elvira Annie Cowles Holmes	June 1843	married	29
Rhoda Richards	June 1843	single	58
Desdemona Caitlin Wadsworth Fullmer	July 1843	single	32
Olive Grey Frost	July 1843	single	27
Nancy Maria Winchester	July 1843*	single	14
Melissa Lott	September 1843	single	19
Fanny Young Carr Murray	November 1843	widowed	56

exact date unknown

OTHER WOMEN SUSPECTED OF BEING SMITH'S WIVES

Sarah Rapson Poulterer

Mary Ann Frost Stearns Pratt

Sarah Scott Mulholland

Phebe Watrous Woodworth

Mary Huston

Olive Andrews

Hannah Dibble

Sarah Ann Fuller

Vienna Jacques Shearer

Jane Tibbets

Aphia Woodman Sanburn Dow Yale

Mary Heron Snider

Hannah Ann Dubois Smith

WIVES WHO LIVED IN SMITH'S HOUSEHOLD AT TIME OF MARRIAGE

Fanny Alger

Louisa Beaman

Eliza Roxcy Snow

Emily Dow Partridge

Eliza Maria Partridge

Lucy Walker

Sara Lawrence

Maria Lawrence

Desdemona Caitlin Wadsworth Fullmer

Melissa Lott

WIVES WHO WERE LIVING WITH THEIR PARENTS AT TIME OF MARRIAGE TO SMITH

Sarah Ann Whitney

Flora Ann Woodworth

Helen Mar Kimball

Nancy Maria Winchester

PAIRS OF WIVES WHO WERE SIBLINGS

Zina Diantha Huntington Jacobs & Presendia Lathrop Huntington Buell

Delcena Johnson Sherman & Almera Woodward Johnson

Emiy Dow Partridge & Eliza Maria Partridge

Sarah Lawrence & Maria Lawrence

PAIR OF WIVES WHO WERE MOTHER/DAUGHTER

Patty Bartlett Sessions & Sylvia Porter Sessions Lyon

WIVES MARRIED TO SMITH WITH EMMA'S APPROVAL

Emily Dow Partridge

Eliza Maria Partridge

Sarah Lawrence

Maria Lawrence

NOTES ON TEXT

This is a work of fiction, inspired by the real polygamous wives of Joseph Smith, founder of The Church of Jesus Christ of Latter-day Saints. It is by no means meant to be read as a biography of the women or a history lesson of the time. For factual information on these women and the history of the Mormon Church, I suggest reading *In Sacred Loneliness: The Plural Wives of Joseph Smith* by Todd Compton and *Mormon Enigma: Emma Hale Smith* by Linda King Newell and Valeen Tippetts Avery.

All italicized sections are from text attributed to the individual women, either from their own writings or quoted by their contemporaries.

Doctrines and Covenants excerpts sourced from: http://www.lds.org/scriptures/dc-testament

The Egyptians referenced in "Zina Diantha Huntington Jacobs" were four mummies Smith bought from a travelling show and claimed them to be a Patriarch and his three wives. At one point he asked Zina Huntington Jacobs to hide them under her bed to keep them safe from the mobs.

In Mormon tradition, in temple-worthy marriages couples marry for both time and eternity. Time, being your time on earth, and eternity being the afterlife. After Joseph's death, many of his wives remarried only for time and were sealed to Smith for eternity.

The mobs were composed of violent non-Mormons. The LDS were a relatively insular group and this, along with their sometimes controversial beliefs, made them targets. There was a history of mobs driving Mormons out of their villages, burning their homes, and tar and feathering the men.

Joseph Smith ran for President of the United States as an Independent in 1844. His campaign ended with his assassination.

The bulk of the poems are set in Nauvoo, Illinois which was the centre of Mormonism from approximately 1839-1844. Many important doctrines of the faith were introduced during this time, including polygamy. After Joseph Smith's death and a succession crisis, Brigham Young took over leadership and the bulk of the population followed him west to Utah where polygamy was practiced openly until 1890. Nauvoo-era polygamy was very different to what was later the custom. It was highly secretive, both polygyny and polyandry were practiced, and polygamous spouses rarely lived together. At its height, only ten percent of the Nauvoo population was polygamous.

While this is a work of the imagination, I consulted many sources in my research. In addition to *In Sacred Loneliness: The Plural Wives of Joseph Smith* by Todd Compton and *Mormon Enigma: Emma Hale Smith* by Linda King Newell and Valeen Tippetts Avery, some important texts were *Rough Stone Rolling* by Richard Lyman Bushman; *No Man Knows My History: The Life of Joseph Smith* by Fawn Brodie; *Nauvoo Polygamy* by George D Smith; *Joseph Smith Portraits: A Search for the Prophet's Likeness* by Ephraim Hatch; *Mormon Polygamy* by Richard S. Van Wagoner; *Women and Authority: Re-Emerging Mormon Feminism* by Maxine Hanks; and *Four Zinas: A Story of Mothers and Daughters on the Mormon Frontier* by Martha Sontag Bradley and Mary Brown Firmage Woodward, plus many other articles, books and internet sites.

ACKNOWLEDGEMENTS

Some of these poems were published earlier as a chapbook, in journals and anthologies. My gratitude to the editors and publishers of each.

Eliza Roxcy Snow, chapbook, rednettle press
"Elvira Cowles Holmes" as a broadsheet for subscriber supplement for *Wonk* No. 5
"Fanny Young" in *Wonk*
"Fanny Alger," "Presendia Huntington Buell," "Martha McBride Knight," "Agnes Coolbrith Smith," and "Marinda Johnson Hyde" in *Unfurled: Poetry by Northern BC Women.*
"Maria & Sarah Lawrence" in *Best Canadian Poetry in English 2011*
"Elizabeth Davis Durfee", "Maria & Sarah Lawrence", and "Delcena Johnson Sherman" in *Event*
"Lucy Walker" in *Branch Magazine*
"Melissa Lott" in *CV2*
"Louisa Beaman," "Nancy Maria Winchester," "Agnes Coolbrith Smith," and "Ruth Vose Sayers" in *Room*

Thank you to the Alberta Foundation for the Arts and Canada Council for the Arts. This book would not have been written without their generous support.

Thank you to the Wallace Stegner House and all those involved with the Banff Centre Writing Studio for giving me space and time to work, and especially Don MacKay for his editorial insight and wisdom.

My deepest gratitude to those who have helped shape this manuscript, particularily Trisia Eddy, Ariel Gordon, and my poetic sister-wives, Laisha Rosnau and Jennica Harper.

Thank you to my publisher, Brian Kaufman. Thank you to Jon Paul Fiorentino for believing in the manuscript. Many thanks to Sarah Sharkey, Karena Dachsel, and Tara Deans who have helped watch the brood to ensure I had a writing-friendly environment. And thanks to my brood—when I started this project there was a brand-new one of you, and now you are three.

And to Kevin, my love, thank you for everything.

ABOUT THE AUTHOR

Marita Dachsel is the author of *All Things Said &
Done* (Caitlin Press, 2007) and the chapbook *Eliza
Roxcy Snow* (rednettle press, 2009). Her poetry has
been shortlisted for the Robert Kroetsch Award for
Innovative Poetry, the ReLit Prize, and has appeared
in many literary journals and anthologies, including
Best Canadian Poetry in English 2011. After many
years in Vancouver and Edmonton, she and her
family have recently relocated to Victoria.